Perceptions of You

Alexis Nicole

Copyright © 2024 Alexis Nicole

All rights reserved. No part of this book may be reproduced or transmitted in any form or by any means, electronic or mechanical, including photocopying, recording or by any information storage and retrieval system without permission in writing from the publisher.

SilverArcher Publishing—Sun Prairie, WI
ISBN: 979-8-218-41888-5
Library of Congress Control Number: 2024908998
Title: *Perceptions of You*
Author: Alexis Nicole
Digital distribution | 2024
Paperback | 2024

Dedication

iii

To my younger self, we made it

Thank you to my support system

Table of Contents

My Thoughts…

Bench

Benches sit waiting for someone to sit
No one here,
No one there,
A lonely bench is
Nowhere near.

We live in a world
run by the economy
where working
is more valued than family
and where money
controls basic needs.

4.19.17

It was a feeling of aching, aching in my chest. As it burned into my brain and I finally knew the truth. It wasn't the act of loving her that kept me going, but the act she put on to make me fall. It was the act of her loving me that drew me in. It was the show of affection that pulled me close. It was the appeal that I got every time she placed her hand on mine. The feeling of tingles through my body like shots from a simple look brought me to life. My legs trembled as I fell to what was known to be the end. As a heart shattered metaphorically. It felt like more than a metaphor, it felt like wounds soldiers came back with from war, fighting for different reasons. Punchers through the skin leaving blood to flow out that no band aid would fix. Nor any medical devices could ever sew back together. That a lifeline had no life to it. As it sat there blank beeping.

You have to manage in a world
full of people, alone.

Written down

My mind takes me places that cannot be written down. That cannot be explained in the use of words. That when writing subconsciously the words vanish into an abyss. Where the picture moving screen slides off as there are no words to be taken in as a feeling. Where it's a place that falls into a place where it is unreachable to any conscious feeling. It's that feeling when your heart flutters as you drift off into space. And you are dreaming of all the things that could be going on. Like a dream you wake up from it's hard to explain what had happened as you spent what felt forever but you can't describe what it exactly looked like, or there were words you were unsure of how to describe. Where a painting is a picture that has no use for words to describe the feeling. As you are unsure how to draw the thing you see in your mind as it moves around but it's untouchable to the earth around you as you have been put into a place that is unreachable to the consciousness of a mind.

Toying around Toys

You toy around with a toy and it might not even be a toy anymore. Your toy could be turned into a thing, an idea, a person, an emotion. You lead it on, you toyed with him for too long. You thought that's all he wanted. You saw the bad in everyone that it turned you to think you were the toy. That they toyed around with you. That you were only being the good toy, the toy that was left on the shelf until picked up to be thrown in a box. And during that they lead you on to leave you in a box. To think they would never come back but they did. They came back to empty the box as the light glistened your skin and brought you back to life over joying in color. To be in their hands at last. You thought you were more this time. You wanted to see the good. You wanted to change the bad in them to good. You wanted to be the one and the only one that could. You didn't want it to be for the girl that was never bought. The girl that was never seen as a toy in his eyes. The toying was never meant for her. You were a practice toy. When a two year old gets their first "phone" that makes different beeps and different ringtones for every time a button is pressed. You were in his grasp that had changed. He didn't toy with you anymore. The flames were rising and burning with more passion than he could ever afford to give to you. He dropped the old ragged toy in, as the flames roared as it was no longer.

12/14/16 Monkey

"What if I told you I was going to kill myself?"
"What?"
The connection was bad.

He was a 15 year old guy.
"What if I did?"

I wanted to cry.
Six Seconds.
That's all it took him.

Done

I'm done. I don't want to hear another thing about my body ever. I don't want fucking compliments. I want to feel hot when I want to. I want to flaunt it off whenever I feel like it because why not. What the hell is wrong with flaunting off your body when you feel like you look good. Another thing to go with that if I am flaunting it off because I want to and you start asking for all this bullshit like "send nudes" I don't want to fucking hear it. I'm doing it because I feel hot. I didn't say you need to say anything. You say I'm a tease well sure am. I don't care if I feel hot that way and I want to show off sometimes. What's wrong with that? What's wrong with loving my body for mere seconds then I have to be reminded that if I want to flaunt it off I'm going to be badgered to send nudes. Or even give blowjobs or sex or whatever in the world everyone wants. Because god forbid I ever try to like myself and show off every once in a while. Even if I'm not flaunting and I want to dress up because I want to feel like I'm pretty I can't because what will happen is they will compliment the dress and later try to get nudes. No not everyone does this but sure is going through their minds. Should that be the goal of all of this? No it shouldn't. I understand if sometimes you are doing it to get somewhere but that isn't always the case. Sometimes you just want to just cause a response of "hey" instead of "I'm gonna wreck" you or send something back. Like yes sometimes I'll want to hear it but most the time that's not what I'm thinking of.

Am I the Problem?

Do you ever feel like you are the problem? That maybe all of your thoughts are ripping and tearing you up on the inside. To where your outsides even become numb. Where you used to be ticklish on the sides of your stomach or where under the knee would make you tense up as someone was trying to tickle you. At a certain point you thought you would lose being ticklish and you wanted the one you loved to be able to get at your points so you no longer liked to be tickled. To where no matter how much you were tickled you still threw your head back in giggles.

Then at the moment when you felt nothing but that you were a molecule floating around to make a whole that was just sitting there, you felt nothing. As he moved over and poked at you like he used to but you felt nothing. You thought maybe you could never be poked at, as he asked "aren't you the ticklish one" then you think about does he remember? Is he talking to other girls and I was nothing to him and I am nothing to him. You sat there with him feeling nothing, not even one giggle slip through, not even a giggle would appear that night. Your body retracted from itself as you shut down, to that molecule built up into a lifeless body.

Hold on love

1 A.M.

Hold on love, as I walk away to never be seen again. As I watch you crumble down to your knees on the middle of the cracked road. You hold my feelings as I had watched you walk away from her once. I saw it coming and you pulled me along on your ride. There is no exit surrounding me as the ride will never end safely.

"There's no more holding on." I spoke softly. I held my head up and walked with long strides.

"I no longer know how to talk to you without an awkward tendency. I don't want small talk anymore. And there is no jumping to the deep end as I would be lost in words that wouldn't even fly around my mind anymore." I watched as you stood there with a blank face as you looked emotionless. As bombs tore you down and all you could do is stand there in silence watching something so horrid but seeing all the little things in the smoke that only you are looking for. Something so small that you cannot find so you take a breath and become emotionless as the smoke is coming closer and covers your body until you no longer can make out that anyone was there.

It hurt more as all I wanted was to get close to you and keep you. You kept me close, closer than anyone ever has. And I threw it away as I broke off the talking at some point as I was preparing not to talk anymore. To detach before it happened so I could walk away and leave in peace as you tried to pretend like it wasn't happening.

Sorry love, I am going home.

False Alarm

It's almost impossible to explain the feeling of falling down. Falling down to your knees where you fall straight through the concrete. Where you tremble in fear of the things around you. As the blur rushes come back to you in a flash. When you cup your hands together and wallow in pain. Your words turn into vacillating breaths. To turn silent as you no longer remember how to breath. Where your head is a spiral of thoughts tumbling down into ruins. To when there is no feeling and you don't know how to cope. Where all you want to do is weep and let out something but you forgot. You forgot how to speak, where you gasp for air but air had been lost a long time ago. Your blood has turned into a stream of peace. Where your heart beat has calmed down to beating so fast per second to a few beats a minute. As you are completely untouchable to the universe around you it's over.

As you are being lifted onto a trolley, a blur of people rush around you moving around in a worry sum look, mouths move as your hearing has become vague. The blur of people become objects fading their color to gray, to black. To where all you can see is black. Where you are now left alone. In your subconscious where you forget everything happening. To thoughts that roam your mind, that you fear, that you love. Yet you can't hear them. As you walk around through a darkness that was never meant to be seen by human eyes you stood before it. You stood before a trapped cage that held a brain and a heart. The heart had risen over pumping blood, as your mind had laid mushed up in the bottom of the cage. As you walked up to the cage, liquid leaked out. Words of all the things you feared were shouting out from your brain that led to a quiet whisper. To your heart barely beating. You punctured a hole through your heart as you watched the blood spill all over your hands and colliding with the remains of the liquid from your brain.

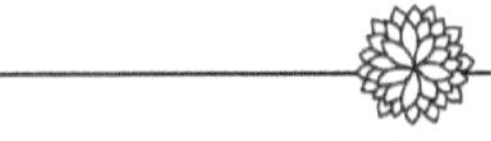

Chained Rhythm

It's when you are alive. Where your body gets jolts of energy. Where you wear nothing but a hat, shirt and undergarment. You follow your feet throughout the house jumping down the stairs as if someone was going to ring your doorbell they would see a body figure move like never before. It's where I stood outside her front door watching as complete silence took over. Headphones swaying back and forth over her see through white long t-shirt. As her hat flew back revealing her face as she tumbled down to get back up. As the music came alive shaking the whole house as her silence moved.

Repeat

There will be a day, when you wake up and start to repeat everything. You will never know when it happens, it will come out of nowhere. And you may never realize when it started to happen. It will be a never-ending habit. It was one of your biggest fears. A fear of giving up and caving in. A fear to never get hurt. A safety zone that was boring, but you no longer know how to escape without having new fears pop up. And soon you realize that you do not know anything else. So then you start to ask different questions to people. They look at you like you are stupid or annoying with how many questions you ask. It was said that there was no stupid question, we all knew that was a lie. But to you some of your questions didn't sound stupid, it was a question of clarification. They have shut you down, and then you are afraid to ask anything more to anyone. You can try explaining things to others that you know, and most just blink it by. You became quiet and quieter not knowing how to talk to others or when too much was said. It was giving up and when you find that something you push it away as it's too good. You don't even consider what is too good for you anymore. You no longer care, you don't think they are too good for you, you have just given up and no longer look to express what's inside.

Sad

It's sad. Everything is sad to you. They way a child smiles, or a baby laughs. It's all just sadness to your heart. It doesn't bring joy, it brings pain. It brings pain of old memories you had when you were that child. When you were happy. Then you see your old best friend, with a guy you used to fall head over heels for. Even when the guy you liked, never talked to you, never gave you the time of day. You see them together and your heart just drops. Your heart sinks so low. Then you remember that you have other people. Those people you mess around with. You lead yourself on by thinking they want you and actually like you. You tease them to your body and you leave them hanging. Like they left you hanging. But they never left you hanging, they were never attached. It was only you living in a fantasy where you thought you could make them fall in love. All you were doing was making them fall for a body that wasn't even so good. You lead them on as you are the "easy" target. You let this happen to yourself as you continue to fall through these traps that they set up.

What is the worst of all is this affects how you do things. You feel like you are not entitled to anything. That you deserve the worst. You feel like you are emotionally detached. That you have all these emotions flying all over but when someone starts to show emotion or anything hard to handle you pull away. You over think what you are made for. That the only way you can ever have someone is to not have them. But to let them have you and use you in any way possible. It brings you up when you get the attention thinking that there is a possibility of someone liking you for your beautiful mind. All the inside features that are not shared with the outside world. Because you have closed down. And it repeats itself every time someone walks into your life you think all they want is your body. And after a while you almost offer it when they pull away. Because it's a habit you were pulled into by the habit you thought you were to others.

Was it ever so wrong to love yourself where in a world it is supposed to be accepted and that's the goal but then they switch it on you and if you love yourself you are judged by cold eyes and shunned out when you get to the point of truly loving yourself. And on your way to truly loving yourself when you have those days that you are in love with yourself people shoot you down or the thought of it lowers you for a mere second. Whenever you get somewhere to the trail of making you happy for a day or days and weeks for something small that you love by either loving how you dance around the house in only a t-shirt or in baggy sweats and you live in the moment. In the moment of music in any moment that is going on you live in it and feel happy. Weather recording yourself or putting makeup on before you go out or even stay in.

Control

It was the thoughts that lingered around my mind, not at night but in the middle of the day. Where daydreams took me to places I had never thought about before. Where my imagination blocked the ability to learn in a classroom. That builds walls cutting people out. That sustained in my mind without noticing. That had more control over me than I did.

Death

There is a love in beauty
that's not spoken within death
but hidden by grief
that's peaceful on the other side

Tension

There is a tension that can't be voided. It's when you walk into the room and our eyes lock. Where my voice trembles when I speak as you made me forget the words leaving my mouth. You speak fluently as if nothing was a worry in the world. To where I wonder if you ever remembered what happened. Where you left me in my place with no other words. With mistakes that once lingered through open doors in my mind that I kept knocking on. Those doors I was knocking on led to your mind. That you broke me down and watched as I suffered right before you. You weren't with me. You were over me.

To see who is looking back
to see the emotions fall from them.
the pain that had lingered
the loss of happiness.
that turned into a silent war
between you,
and them-

There's no feeling
of love
or numbness
happy is just an illusion
how have you had this pull
that has made love
but love doesn't exist?
how am I supposedly happy
but with no feeling of it
there is no feeling
but it's not numbness

There's a coldness
a coldness not even the hottest temperature on the shower will warm
not the blankets you cuddle up in with
as your body tingles with numbness
the water pouring down
where the only feel you have is your hair pulling down
the water hitting your head is invisible to you
a touch of anything cannot be felt
numb-
that's what they call it
but maybe you are more than numb
maybe you are cold.
the type of cold that cannot be warmed.
the chills sent through your body
sitting in front of the fire you still feel that coldness you have felt once
before
that drifted on for days,
weeks,
months
that would not go away.
you would rather be numb,
and when you are numb,
you'd rather be cold.
and when you are cold
you wish it would stop.
never ending this cycle you were pulled into.

It's that point
where your untied converse lay on the ground
where your color pencils are dull
where the lack of intelligence stands strong
where your favorite songs have no impact
where the field you used to love
where your words no longer bring you to life
That's when you know.

Six Seconds.

You pulled the trigger.
you bleed through.
you hung.
you took your life.

you're gone.
your mind-
your soul-
your presence.

your body.

your body laying on the ground,
your body lying in the bath, with the water still running
your body hanging from that rope.

your life,
your future,
you-

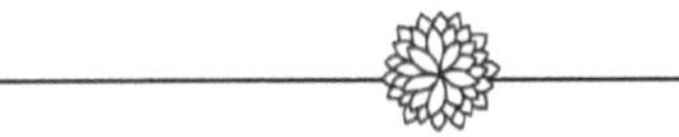

Hurricanes
as they surround you
your grasp of air descends-
as another replaces it

to escape
from the flames
that were stored inside.

as we break through towering walls,
like the shanghai tower

craving the impossible;

of you-
of me-
of us--

left in an untold fairy tale
adrenaline rushes
as we are unfinished

9:30pm
3:27am
you and I

one step
hand in hand

In a crowded room
where its loud
yet silent.
as mouths move around;
forming words
or smiles
or connecting with others,

you see it in others,
how they feel.
the sleepy eyes
the pain in their throat
as they move along
as no one watches.

It's the silent screams
that are forced to be the loudest
the ones that bring pain
and suffrage to one
where your body feels the pain
as you pull at your hair
to try and make it go away

A Letter to You

You have been here for a while
as I wrote before
you have ceased to exist
a figment of my imagination
to bring me to a peace
a therapy of my own
that many have followed
but you weren't why I was sad
you just helped express thoughts
and I'm letting you go

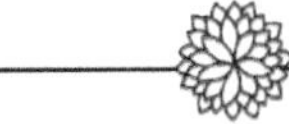

Car Crash

As it hit you spirals were formed from the impact.
your hands were tingling,
your heart racing
as your vision went black.
with a hand placed on your thigh,
a reassuring voice
asking if you are okay
as if nothing had happened
as a stranger has appeared
oblivious to the damage done.

College is where memories are made. I have some friends that I can talk to, but when you don't drink you feel left out. And when you do drink you get drunk fast as you don't have a tolerance yet. There's more to do than drink and I have always said that. But I feel into it, the typical college student. Drink on the weekend and feel the hangover the next day. And it sucks when in the morning you're all alone puking with no one by your side. And you wake up and realize you have no one. Maybe it's the one time you have no one but you wake up as you feel like dying and everything hurts. And you just want someone to give you tender love and raise you up. But instead you wake up after hours of feeling horrible and you have to manage in a world full of people, alone.

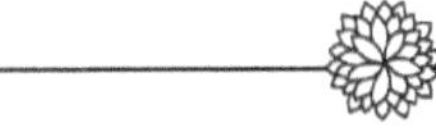

Dissolved Paper

"3...2...1" A ripping from my mouth brought a sharp pain to my gums and lip. They had given me four shots that had made me numb. When the numbness wears off the next day a white dissolved thing appeared in my mouth. It looked like dissolved paper. Where it had been sitting in your mouth for a while and your saliva had formed around the paper. It might have been skin, the taste of the metal blood that washes your mouth when you get hurt. The paper looks smoothed over with a glossy glare. Feels like an extra layer added, that holds small bumps in every area of the paper. It brings up the flesh whenever you move your mouth. Your teeth scratch the surface when the flesh is moved up. Tearing at the attached falling apart skin. The back of that one tooth that caused all of this is rough. Is rough with that fake filling they gave you so you wouldn't have to extract the actual tooth. Where your lips come together so close as the words you speak form from the air seeping through the small slits your lips leave. As it starts to spread where your breath of words turns to mumbles behind sealed lips.

Free and Gone

It's where you have read everything about fake people. It's where you have friends that always leave. And you have thought about this many times and your friends have never done it to you. They have been with you so long they have turned into family members. That you do fight but you regain it because you care about them and they care about you. Then when you hit a point they say you are not worried about their problems. When you are but you have yourself to worry about as well. You realize that they are putting this all on you, when you have your own issues. That's when you start to figure out what they are doing. They do not care about you and you tell them that. And they say they care. But if they cared they would not make it harder on you. They said they understand what you're going through but others don't think that. It's where they are more worried about themselves where they try their best to make you feel guilty about it. When all you were trying to do was improve yourself in a subject like school. And that school was supposed to be prioritized above other activities you have joined. You do not feel guilty about it. You feel hurt as you have just lost something that mattered to you. It's not fully lost but you are thinking about fully losing it. But how could you fully lose it when for years and years that is all you grew up with. It's a habit that gets broken with others very fast. But this habit was good to you for so long. And then the habit has grown up and is trying to destroy you with no care. It's something that makes you think. Think about all the times it has been going on when you have felt like this before. This is the ending point that you have to let go. It's time for you to leave, start over. As everyone is holding on with death grips, you must slip through it. You are now free. And they are gone.

Air

It's when you breath. Where your lungs open. Where you lean your head back as you feel it all around you. Where it stains down your throat making a path from your open mouth to your lung. Where the air is fresh bringing you to life, as you have always breathed it. It's different than the last. You can taste the air, feel it moving within your body. Where you can see the little path of air moving straight to you. As it enters you can hear the rush going to calm as you close your mouth. As it smells like something you haven't smelt. Not the smell of the bakery goods your mom makes in the morning, or the smell when you get roses or walk into nature. It's not the smells of a dumpster truck passing your house or the smell of diesel gas. It's a smell that doesn't have a name. It doesn't smell good nor bad, it's not neutral but a word that has not been created. It has been found before and touched in that way but they left it without a word. To bring the emotion to you when you finally find your air. When it's a discovery of your own to find it and it leaves you taking in all that breath to leave you breathless.

Hobbies

There may be a point in life where you hit sadness. And you feel alone in the darkest points. You feel nothing high of yourself and give up total hope. When they ask you what you do for fun and you have nothing to say. Where others have found their hobbies. Doesn't mean they are happy, but they are one of the lucky ones who finds something they enjoy. For the rest of us we are lost. And to find something we could remotely enjoy would cost money. The money we can't afford to lose on something to possibly make us feel happy. But beyond having that, we push through and keep moving on, feeling sad, numb, depressed. Tired of everything and back to being lost. Happiness is just a word that has no meaning and is lost yet again. But happiness doesn't belong to a hobby. Some of us will realize that when you go through your everyday life doing the same old thing, wake up to a job, to coming home and watching repeats of shows because nothing else interests you. You ponder so much because you are happy but so lost. Sometimes you almost wish to be sad just to feel something more and blame it on something.

Sniffles

Do you ever just feel like you can't. When you're sitting down in a classroom as a teacher gives his/her lecture where you need to blow your nose but you can't. You can't because its silent and you feel like blowing your nose will be loud. You can't because you feel awkward standing up to get a tissue that's nearly only 10 feet away. You can't because you feel awkward with doing anything in silence or when it's not quiet but it's not loud where to the point you can blow your nose or sniffle the rest in. Or if you need to go to the bathroom but you don't want to raise your hand and wait for the teacher to call on you so you can ask with your stuffed nose to go to the bathroom, or because they are rambling and you don't find it worth asking to go. And when you do you feel weird and all that pressure goes to you but when you are out of the class you are fine.

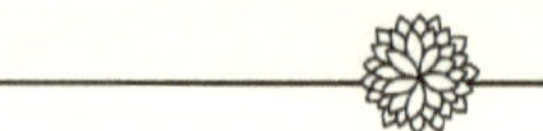

If words are letters assembled together,
what are letters when they are assembled
to not make a word?
If letters are just sounds pronounced
different ways.
to sound different coming from a mouth
to make different sounds that don't have letters?

About Him…

Him

The way he smiles,
as dimples appear
at the corner of his lips.

the way his pants sag
as they simply don't fit.

maybe the play fighting.
where when he moves me-
so gently,
I can't feel I'm moving.

maybe how his arms wrap around me,
how he holds me when we cuddle.

how my hands fit perfectly in his.
the way I nestle my head on his chest

the way his voice is deep,
and in the mornings
like a cold or scruffs.

"Regrets?" he asked.
    I have a lot.

Bubbly bashful butterflies batted and blushed as he walked by.
his smile bright as night.
am I invisible to him?
then his eyes met my gaze,
and my heart soared into the sun,
and a new life awoke.

Prairie Voices

They covered her body
it ran through her bloodstream,
her bones dipped into it-
drenched.
hands that tinkered around
for the use of your satisfaction
clenching to you
to be held.
You let go
to be free
from the fear
she brought.

from yourself-
to grow
without the soul
that knew all of yours.
to hold
the dust created
for your fears
to sorrow

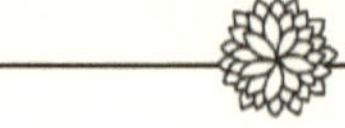

Psychological

The nights I have cried myself to sleep.
to the nights where I can no longer see.
the nights where I can't even cry.
staring emotionless at the wall.

where my emotions were stolen.
stollen farther beyond depression.
some call it numb,
others have no words.

to describe something so painful
where there is no such thing
that exists in only some
but those are the left ones.

the ones left behind
to wallow
to suffer

where their existence doesn't exist to them anymore.
for unknown reasons
psychological?

Repeated

There is this dream that I have had over and over and over.
there are similar dreams to it.
such as there is a chase.
to others, they say it's just a dream.
or I have had nightmares like it,
and I've repeated nightmares.
I no longer remember the start,
but the end.

it ends like this

he was chasing me.
a relationship?
a killer?
the joker?

through tall old brick buildings
jumping rough to rough
shinny dim street lights
flickering on and off.

no sounds in the street
and no one in sight.

the gun
and the chase

there was a ledge
next to a brick wall.
this is where the dream ends
face to face with the gun and him
he stood far away but yet so close
I have never encountered him once in these dreams
besides the echoing face that floated near me a couple times

"At that moment I should have left."
   "Why didn't you?"
   "Because I still love you." She turned around and walked away.

About I…

I was never prepared
maybe because
I never planned to be here this long
but here I am
and maybe I never looked hard enough
for resources I needed
and never took advantage
but I seek for other help and was shot down
I spent so much time being shot down
just for trying to improve my education
but they send you to other people
who send you to others
in a cycle because no one has time to deal with it
and it never helped.

The tears are fading away
as the numbness left
and the alcohol had started
and when it started I lost the fight
of caving in

How can you run away from something
if you're the thing you're running from

Hurt

It's a hurt where it corrupts your body
where you scratch and tear at your body
and it hurts to hold back
to want to hurt yourself
is so cruel.
but it's all I can feel

I don't see myself in this world with you anymore
and I don't see you anymore

I thought it was going to be different.
I thought you were going to be different.

a light shown above that night
one that took me away.
took me into your arms.

I was as cold as a foggy breath
as you laid me down
and touched my skin

for the first time my body jittered.

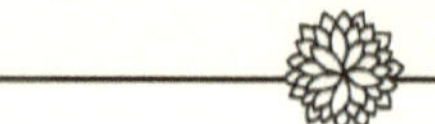

I was never prepared
maybe because
I never planned to be here this long
but here I am

Uncancerous Cancer Ball

It's there
it came out of nowhere
the little marble shaped ball-
that moved around in its given space
where it popped out sometimes
like if you raised your arm,
a half of a circle that just popped out.
You knew it wasn't supposed to be like that
you hated the sight-
the feel
yet you hated the idea.
the idea that it moved in your body.
that the thought of it could be more
that it would alter your life.
and every time you looked down,
or brushed passed it with your hand-
you flinched, cringing your body,
this little marble shaped ball has shaped your life,
you had to be careful.
thinking what could be,
if it never happened.
it hasn't happened and you know that
the thought still lingers around,
and that's what you fear

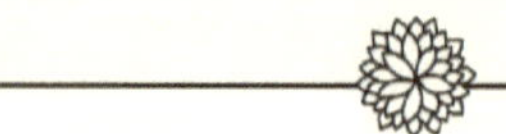

And maybe I never looked hard enough
for resources I needed
and never took advantage
but I seek for other help and was shot down
I spent so much time being shot down
for trying to improve my education
but they send you to other people
who send you to others
in a cycle because no one has time to deal with it
and it never helped

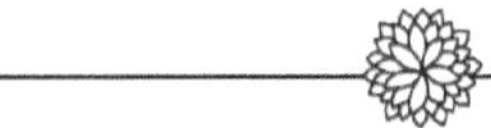

I'm only feeling sad
because I'm alone,
and I make sure I'm alone
by pushing you away,
and by hating myself
more and more,
as life goes on
and I'm growing
the wrong way.

I used to love myself
but my eyes are opening up
and I can see everything
that I don't want to see

If I had a daughter…

Dani, Charlie or Blake.
she will be like the solar system.
as she dances around.
gliding on blue and purple rays
that shine bright around her

earth will be heartless,
the sun will be warm
Venus will be hyperborean.
accepting all in her way.

meteors will destroy her
like humans without air.
the stars will surround her
as she picks up the remains.

the air around her will become
unbreathable.
with nothing to save her
she will come home.

to me,
to her father
where she knows it's okay.
she will lay down
as her adventures end and remember.

My face might be known by society
but my mind is hidden within the earth
and the thoughts are captivated.

It made sense
to disappear
within a depressant
to fade away
and forget the problems
of being alone.
to sober up
brings reality
that the support
was never there
and you leaned
into darkness

It's painful within death
that's hidden by grief
that's peaceful on the other side

The first time-
it was for four years.

the chase-
is forever-

every day seeing you-
to maybe never again-

holidays for now-
until it's real.

text messages grow faint-
yelling down the stairs stops.

the best bedtime stories,
are no longer.

when we had sleepovers
laying in your bed singing-
until mom and dad came home.

to when I started cooking for myself-
dashing for my room-
no contact with a soul.

I wish I would have known our time was ending.

I would have taken more pictures.
I would have played more games.
I would have been there.
instead I was not.

I lay here without you.

without singing-
laughing-
crying-
emotion.

the walls have never looked more blank.

I need you to understand
that I am only here for one reason
you know that reason by heart

I know you do not want to
and you may want more
but you know why I am this way

you know it will only be for pleasure
that beyond any thought
I am already gone

you know I want it differently
but it cannot be changed
no matter how hard you try and force it

it's a habit that I have fallen deep into
that I am incapable of the thought
of anything different

and if I could I'd go back and do it over
I would change every moment
with the least regrets in the world.

and who I am right now will change
if you let yourself change
then I could be released

but it's the last thing you can do
I need you to understand.

Something I no longer have
is the mind I used to
the one where thoughts flow freely
and accessible adventure was found

something I no longer have
is dignity
ripped from within
deeper than one's findings

something I no longer have
is free will within myself
where dancing around like a child
is unacceptable in society

something I no longer have
is the numbness that had lingered around
rather than being sad
and letting walls fall down

something I no longer have
nor have ever had
was the love I wanted
from you, and only you

something I no longer have
is the worries about being me
that has led into acceptance
with my surroundings

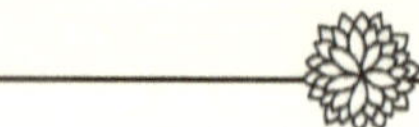

I have not been in this world long enough
but I've been here realizing it wasn't meant to be
and that maybe some of us are better off
left in our thoughts
with the few loved ones
but never finding the right one

I've always imagined
a perfect body
and personality
for myself
so boys would like me
and I'm sitting here
with my heart dropped
because of it.

I said I'd never drink
and then my heart dropped

it ruined my mind
my motivation
it left me empty

I thought I had everything
figured out
planned out
I know I didn't think far ahead
but my mind
is damaged
and can't be taped back together
this time

I'm homesick
but I have no home

It's weird how little nibbles don't get me. or kisses and showing love in that way. How just talking and playing around can bring the same things. How the idea of big gestures is amazing but not knowing how to deal with that. But too long for the need of talking and to never stop over someone kissing you. Has never been important. Sure I like it and don't ever want it. but I could live without it and be peaceful.

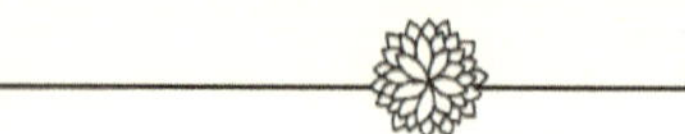

It's when you sit in a emotionless puddle
that all your fears come rushing back.
when the hardest part is over
when you no longer feel the pain
where the numbness is lost
and there's no going back
to hitting the point
it's the crashing waves
that are said to be agonizing.
that when you are at your high
it's excruciating
the worries of the world are dropped
you are released
you're free to slouch your back with no judgement
you're free to the donuts on the table
that you so ever resisted
from the fear of others
from the fear of judgement
from the fear of you~
and the thoughts that constantly linger through your head
the new thoughts that you can enjoy
and the old to brush off
as if they had never existed
as if pain is just a word,
that brings no harm.

I know I'll keep putting myself in situations
where I shut down
but I was taught that
and I'll learn to get out one day
but I think when I find my new you
they will make me forget
and take my pain away
and that's when I will learn
it's okay to feel comfortable around my you
instead of you shutting me down
and making me look for you
and getting hurt

I've been waiting for you
to come back to me
but you stayed a lost thought
and I cannot find you
I wish I never throw you out
because in this world
you were all I knew
and you knew me

This hurts
where I have to be scared
living, breathing
where I have to be so secure because of what you have done
Where I have to double check everything-
to make sure it's not you
not you slipping through the cracks
I cannot leave anything behind
so you can trace me
no matter how hard you try
I will be gone one day
because of you
I have to live my life in fear
not fearing more…
I don't know where it will stop
or if it will ever end
it's sad
because I know this isn't happening to just me...

Body confidence
is something I used to understand
that seems so unrealistic now
I used to hate my body.
I hated it for not having any boobs
and then to when asses came into play
I had gotten the breasts I was happy with.
then worried about the back.
I was happy with my body
no matter what anyone said I was happy
it was then when the closets of friends
had said I was like a rectangle
that hit me harder than anything
now all I see is the number on the scale
that I would have been fine with
but now no matter numbers
all I see is an empty rectangle.

But maybe if they would actually help me. Like in math they keep saying they will listen but they don't. I told them I need help, that I go out of my way to find help asking any teachers but when I ask teachers they won't help and I don't need it in all of my classes but when you sit down and look at the evidence it's right in front of you. It's in the papers. Look at the test grades I will go from a D to an A when I sit down and talk it out. There is tremendous evidence that I do on my own out of my way but they keep putting roadblocks in the way. It doesn't help that I'm alone either sure every once and awhile I find someone new to "Play" with but does it last? No it doesn't because for whatever reason I won't let people get close with me. I push them out or even if I don't I get "sick" of them maybe? Like there is not a chase and I crave that chase of having something. I crave the chase that isn't real but I want to make it real but it's impossible because I set it to be impossible. Not as it's not obtainable but the actual chase is impossible such as that's the word I'm chasing after in things the impossible and the imagination of it.

And I wasn't happy anymore
I had an emotion I didn't know what it was
like I had no emotion at all
but not feeling all of the emotions
like they came crashing at me
it was nothing
because I felt it

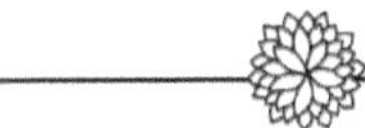

I think I have lost my voice
that writing won't even bring back
like it's tied up inside of me
so deep that it cannot be found
and it happened from past experiences
that I have found peace with.
but even with peace, it had caused damage
and that damage can't be healed

October 28 2018, 12:34 A.M.

I have yet to find my purpose
and it scares me that I won't find it

I wanted to stop existing on this earth.

About Her...

Irrelevant

10/26/16

"I just had the weirdest dream about you," she said.

"What?" I replied.

I looked at her and couldn't grasp my heart. The things that I could tell her would break her. The things that happened in reality when she was lost in a gaze. She was too innocent. I could not crush this for her. When she spoke, light glowing from her shone all over, as the city behind her burned and lit up in flames.

She rose and danced around me, she then took my hand and pulled me along. "It all happened in a forest! You were there, a castle deep in the forest, where the Russians were preparing for battle. There was snow on the ground about four feet high. The castle looked like it was built from concrete."

As she spoke and took me along, snow started to fall and tall jungle trees arose. In the distance a castle appeared, I looked back to see the city that was once in flames turn to ashes. The whiff of the breeze made me shiver. Completely surrounded with snow and trees we were gone.

1/2/17

It happened. It happened in a way I couldn't explain, like the way people made up different things or lived in different time periods. Where time seemed irrelevant. Where in that moment there was no one, not like a cliché where you say we were the only people left. But in a way where subconsciously there was nothing. Where the unknown takes place. Weather you linger around with no meaning, where you lay in the ground and rot or if there is something more, like heaven or hell. Either way it happened. I could feel the pain he felt when it happened. He just watched the only person he loved die. Fly out a shattered car window. Hit the ground and laid there. He was silent. Almost like someone reached in and sucked the warmth out of his body, to the touch everything was numb. Where even in the blizzard of snow didn't feel so cold yet just another thing happening in that moment. As the sirens came from all over it just looked like an ambulance with flashing lights. Where sound was oblivious, where air was unbreathable, and seeing was just an illusion.

The sadness that had left her
she lost a part of herself
that no one could understand.

I stopped loving her. It wasn't because she was sad. She had a past. Her past was 7 years long. It was something only she could understand as she went through it. You could have an idea but it happens differently to everyone. She got better, and after that, that's when I found her. She was outside of the movies. It wasn't a play by play, nor was it the stories where you found adventure with the love of your life. It was with someone who was happy, who moved passed being numb. There were days where you questioned moving passed being numb, as you weren't sure you were really happy. It was the little things that I couldn't get over. The way you non stopped talking when you brushed your hair. The excitement when your song came on. Where in moments we did live in the movies. Where we had a perfect time together. It was never your bad luck that made me stop. You were happy and full of love, never to selfish unless it was the corner spot of the couch. You had a beautiful soul, that you never got around to sharing. It was hard for you to speak, and share thoughts. You had them but your wording never fit. You never thought you were smart. You had many issues that some were ignored. It wasn't the strangers in your head. There was no explanation of why I left you. Not that you could ever figure out yet. You had ideas, maybe because you got annoyed too fast, or you got lazy. Loud sounds you couldn't stand. You wish you found your piece but you focused on small things for too long. You thought that you were better, and maybe you are. You're lost in a world with no guide. You thought you talked too much about yourself and you tried to care for others. You never knew how to talk to new people, or how you would ever get the same relationship. It broke your heart when you had no one for one of the most important things in your life. Where celebrating hurt. You felt like a bother to anyone you started talking to. You couldn't tell who started to care or who wanted nothing. They toyed with your mind for so long. That it became a habit that led to even worse habits. The fear you had of being alone and what could happen. You couldn't even stress eat because when you got sad you stopped eating. You were fine with your body but everything made you stray away. You were upset that you never even liked many foods. It held you back from adventures. You didn't mind being picky but you picked out all your flaws. You became content and you strived for others to know you were okay. You made everyone think you are okay. You even convinced yourself. And you can never get out of that convincing. You pushed out loved ones because you couldn't understand. The was never the issue.

But I'm toying with your mind forever, and you will never figure out why I stopped loving you.

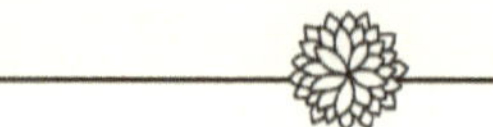

4.18.17

"I just had the weirdest dream about you." He just sat there and stared out in the distance. "It's where you were genuinely cared. It was when she wasn't in your existence yet. Where you would fall over and over for me like you used to before she showed up. It was when you would start singing for me in the middle of a crowd and you watched me dance around. You were finding yourself in every piece of me instead of me falling hard like I did."

"It was a letter to you that I wrote. I watched you fall, and I let you hit the waters where you couldn't reach the bottom." He spoke soft, fiddling with his hands.

"In the dream…" he looked down then up at me, "you felt okay. I watched you fall for me. You were going on exotic whims, you didn't care about the world around you all you could do was see me. That's all you ever wished for…"

"I had those bad thoughts when I was with you that went away when I found her. I can look at her and fall in love whenever she moves her mouth. And when she smiles and she doesn't notice the world around her, that's all I have ever wanted. With you? I was never there. I never listened to you nor did I ever care. I don't care about your dream. That's not why I came here."

"It was the end…" He got up and grabbed his jacket then walked away. "You finally said you loved me…."

It was the tears
that poisoned her
the tears
that drowned her
that took her under
and held her
until she could forget

She created a world
one to be free
to forget about the sad
to ignore numb
where you felt something
that wasn't sad or happy
to not be content
but to live and have a soul
even if it was to forget
she would smile at others
and say hi while passing strangers
she wouldn't stay up crying
or have sleepless nights
she was at peace

I stopped loving her.
she was sad once
and she showed me her.
she was a beautiful damaged soul
she opened a new world
that was full of life and love,
she was a stranger to the dark
she roamed around without a name.
she was free.

there were no limits
her world was not met for two
it was for her to blossom

but she never reached the end

I wish I could love her
and her is you.

Silhouette

As she sat in the back, if the light of him.
as the rest had watched her,
her beauty that she led off.
her beautiful mind that she spilled out in her writing,
in the paintings that she had destroyed.
as a beautiful young girl
who had fallen head over heels,
for a boy who wouldn't give her the time of day.

Her love had torn me apart. She was the best thing that had ever happened to me. I was sad before I had met her. I understood her in ways no one else could even see. It could have been the way I treated her to make her stay. Spoiled her in every way I could. I gave her all my love and attention. I had never worked on getting to know myself when I was around her. I couldn't think straight. The way she had that pull on me. When she would dance around me in public like no one was watching. She was never able to do that before. She could walk around anywhere like we were the only ones. She was alone without me. She had opened up and got comfortable to where the things she had done on her own, she incorporated me into them. Her love was vibing off of her and spreading. She didn't hesitate to be lazy some days, then wake up other days and explore the world. She had shown me that there was hope in more than just us. That she never thought she was going anywhere in the world, she was too shy. Her personality lit up every time she was left alone. She could be free to express herself. With me she didn't care if she didn't sound as sophisticated. There was a trust and comfort that was built up. To express every thought that went into her head. Even if she had gotten bored of talking and there was nothing to do. The most random of things and all the what if's that could go on. She didn't care, she was freed. She had found herself and she wasn't sad anymore. She had been content, all that's all she had ever wanted. Maybe that's why I left her when she still had my heart. She is always with me and remembered.

Letters to You…

I started using you as my insperation

Not that I ever noticed.
nor that I paid attention

I knew the little things
that you did
and I loved it dear

and you had all the room you could
but you had all the wrong reasons

It never left my mind
once you took me there
a beautiful place
full of rain
and full of life
a place eye opening
to the beautiful, sad,
that was so uplifting

My heart drops at the thought of you.
I shut down my emotions towards you.
as you never had the capacity.
all you ever wanted was to be pleased
as your desires fell into your lap.

as you watched them crawl and beg
for the attention they handed off for you.
for you to look at them as a tiny speck
running around to your every need.

to never have the chance
to make yourself an emotionless creature
and only to find you are no longer my problem
that felt like a million stabs when you had vanished.

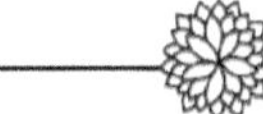

I said yes
and lost to temptation
to be like the others
and fit in,
to feel something
that everyone loved
and it wasn't right
how I gave myself away to a stranger
who just left
and it's because I wasn't in the right
I wasn't in the right state of mind
and I said I never would
but I didn't want to let you down.

I want to love you with all of my heart, but you have to understand my past. I could share all of it with you, but it would take a lifetime and there would be no future. I want you to forget my past. I want you to look past the inconveniences that occurred. I want you to know that I have accepted my past and I have come to peace with it. I have also come to peace with who it made me today. I understand that I am a tease, that I am afraid to let you in. I will want to dance around you in public. I will want to look like a crazy in love fool. And I want you to prove me wrong that I'm not a fool for what I have chosen. I will want you to open me up in a way I never thought possible. I want it to be the thing they call "goals" and I want you to be the one I can tell anything to. I want to spoil you and let you see the love that I feel. I may feel it but be speechless about it. I won't ever be able to describe how in love with you that I will be. Those are words that will never be created nor ever thought of. They are words that cease to exist.

You are now my spot
my spot that I could nezzle down in
where my breaths come to calmness
where the gross little black hole
is just on the side far enough
that I didn't have to worry about touching it
where my body sinks into you
and you take my worries away
where I could come to relax or work
with blocking out the outside world
where my dreams could come true
and time became irrelevant

Getting close to you scares me more than ever
I push and I go until I know there no fixing it
I don't know why I do
it's been a tendency
and it's all I know at this point
and at some point I know I need to let go
of the past
but the past has made me who I am
and I'm scared of that
I'm scared I was meant to be alone
for the better of myself
and I've been comfortable this way
and breaking that down
I don't know when I'll be ready
and it's been 7 years since I was myself
but now this is who I am
and I haven't learned anything else
and maybe my wish to be with you
isn't what I want
and I wish it to feel normal
but maybe my normal is being by myself
with no partner
but still having connections with others

His eyes were cold and lifeless as he stared into mine.
his hands were steady as he wrapped gauze around my leg.

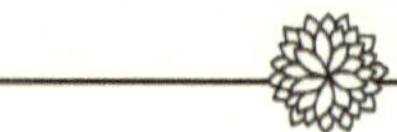

You taught me there were more,
more "bad guys"
you strayed me away from the good,
so you could be a protector.
lied to me to hold on a little longer-
then ran away so I would chase
to leave to someone worse
to keep me in a never-ending loop
that you placed in my head

I want to understand you
and understand why you are so silent
and why you could never let anyone in
when all I ever wanted was to have you
to have you let me in
I wanted to love you
and to receive that back
and it bothered me more than ever
that I coped with figuring myself out
and maybe I'm in the process of finding myself
but once I wanted to let you in
I wanted your feedback
but all you were capable of doing
was grabbing my body
pulling me in closer
to make out
like you never cared about my words
but wanted to shut me up
and that's how you silenced yourself
and maybe that's who you are
you keep it in
or there isn't anything to share

but that's why I want to understand
because it's driving me crazy
and thinking I'm the problem
so please enlighten me
and explain how you got into my heart
and broke it with doing nothing

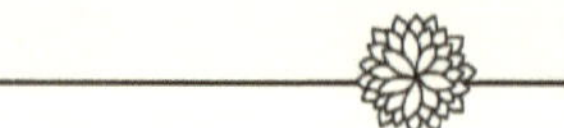

It's the late nights that I never had with you, where the car rides with blasting music and the windows down and our eyes had meant. They meant like they never had before and it was in that moment I had realized that you were more than I could ever imagine. That behind the surface and the artificial acts there was more to you. It was those days that I had never got with you. It was the days that you were at the games in the bleachers leading the crowd because you sprained your ankle and were out of sports for the last year of high school. It was when you were hugging me and flaunting me off to all of your buddies when I wasn't in the room. It was those moments I had never experienced with you. It's when you were alone that she was right for you. All along instead of me it was her, and when you left her and had been alone for some time- that's when you realized she was me. By that time I had already experienced my own artificial love. It was a boy who never saw through me and I settled for it. It was a path that should never have started but with her it did.

You make me want to dance with my eyes open
where I don't have to imagine dancing correctly
where you don't mind my imperfections
you make me want to have someone around
where now you have seen me
and I can be let free.

You say I'm different
and I know I am.
I'm different from the girls you know
but I'm not far from most
I'm different with who I am
but not the action I take
I hold much more
but I give away
I push it away
so you grab it and you love it
but when I show you I'm different
you throw me away
and run
to the ones
who stay the same

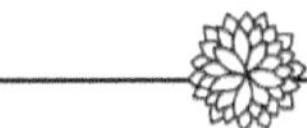

You started sounding different
the quivers
that spilled out
as you tried to speak
words couldn't flow out
your mouth was shaking
as you were shivering
when you let go
and it was all over

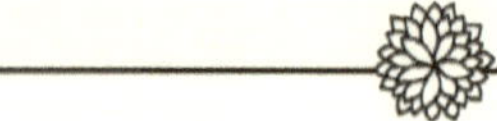

Open
arms,
mind,
heart,
warm
hugs,
thoughts,
home
&
you

Why can't you see me?
spinning round and round in circles
trying to let you know
that I've been here
waiting,
for you to be ready
and to catch me when I get to dizzy
but you can't see me falling
when she's standing still.

I know to look for you
and others like you
but I don't know them
and I'm unknown
my thoughts will never be captured
and when they are learned
I'll know when to stop hurting
and when to stop chasing
the ones who are like you

We didn't ask for this
it just happened
it was great at first
and then you tried to scream it away
you couldn't get it to stop
and everyone thought it was amazing
you could handle it
unless it got too big
and you wanted to be a kid
and scream and kick
to get it away
it tore you apart
and had you sobbing
and loss of breath
and it was out of your control.

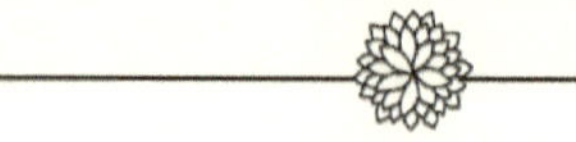

Label

You were happy.
then they gave us a label
I liked the label
you didn't.
so you gave me a label of my own.
you ran me over,
tied me down,
shot me from the sky,
all because of your label.
why would you do that?
didn't you care?
Silly, Shy, Sweet, safe.
was how you described me.
then you made these labels to make yourself grow.
I saw it on the walls,
my heart sank lower than the sun sets into the water.
then his eyes met my gaze,
my heart soared into the sun
and a new life awoke.

I don't taste sweetness
with you gone
the butterflies are gone,
and replaced with chills
you turned sour
when you disappeared
and you're nowhere to be found

It's the sex you want
that fills your body in awe
and butterflies…
maybe.

you speak of wonders
and how your body is
filled with pleasure
that you want with me.

it's all you have ever seen with me
you have seen a nude body
that you no longer call art
but a sexual desire

to me it's the way you move your lips
and flutter your eyes
it's the love that I see
that goes beyond the skin

the love that is real
the love that has been shot
with burning arrows
that brings unforgiving flames.

and the unforgiving flames
tare you apart
that you are only filled
with that one sexual pleasure

you have no care of throwing it away
as it makes you "happy"
when you know you can have more
and it's laid out for you.

I'm scared.
I'm scared it's you when the number pops up
when I don't see a name

I'm scared it's you
coming back
to haunt me
to torture me

when you don't answer when I ask who it is
when you take a long time-
I'm scared it's you and not them

you put me on lockdown
where I no longer feel safe
in my body
in my thoughts

I never know if it will be you

I'm scared to pick up the phone when an anonymous number calls
I'm scared to go downstairs fearing they know
I'm scared to let anyone know you exist
or do you exist-

you have to be real
you are not made up
a figment of imagination
you are real

what you do is real.
to hurt someone
to haunt
to do what you do
is inhumane.

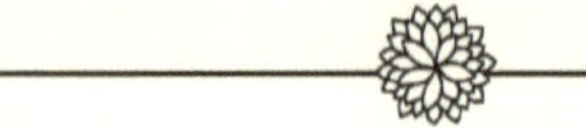

The way his eyes shine
like there is light beaming-
to make a bright glow.

You're not here now
and I don't know who you are
but we will run into each other
I'll stop searching
and I'll stop waiting
because I know you're coming

I'm not supposed to blame you
but I'm lost without you
and I know I didn't get here on my own
but it sure feels like I'm alone right now
and that there is no more drowning
or flying
the numbness left
and I'm sitting in this world
more lost than I was with you

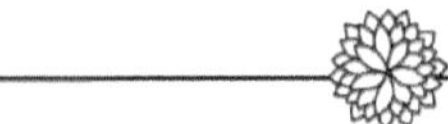

I have not been in this world long enough
but I've been here realizing it wasn't meant to be
and that maybe some of us are better off
left in our thoughts
with the few loved ones
but never finding the right one

I'm afraid
I won't find you
and it will be too late
I'm afraid
I will grow old
and you'll be missing
I'm afraid
that you will never find me
and it will be the last chance

You decided to have fun with me. That's all you were ever looking for, you put this act on for everyone around you and you played your part. You presented the show to me, to find out that all shows have an ending and reality comes next. The pushing never worked, the force came too hard and I couldn't carry it. You led all of these problems from your back to me. You didn't want anything that came with it but the sexual appeal that I never let seep in. You crawled around and tinkered with your hands as much as you could plant in.

I don't want to call you
You.
I don't think you deserve that
and I don't think you know how much
you have hurt me
and how much you took from me
I don't think you know you did something wrong
I don't think that you've gotten better
and today you scared me
I've seen you around and have held it in
but today you said hey Lexi
and I didn't know who it was
until I turned and I tried being nice
but how I was shaking
I think you know
and I don't know why you did that
I know you may try and be a good person
but I don't think I will ever ignore it
and I will always remember

I've never been able to open up
and I've blamed you for so long
for taking something from me
that I was never ready to give you
and I blamed your actions
for stripping me down
of my own will

It's not a thank you
as I will never forgive you
but I'm not going to blame myself anymore
I'll never know when my moment is
but I can assure you I will rise up
and you will never hold me back again.

Me: "Did you ever love me?"

Him: "Yes."

Me: "Do you still?"

Him: "No."

Outsiders: "Why do you push people out?"

Me: "Because there once was a boy who I loved and he stopped one day and took my heart with him without return."

Outsiders: "So why does that make you push people away?"

Me: "Because I can't bear a mistake like that again."

Love

Don't come close
don't pretend you will love forever
as it's a temporary love
not to pass time
but to feel something again
to love with your heart
and to hold it
and when it's over
you will be whole
with a burning love
as you had moved on to your one love
the love that holds something more
that you needed to be whole

You have my legs trembling
as my knees fall to the ground.
as you tower over me and take control
as I drown in the pond of tears surrounding you.

as you sink down to my level
with no more magic in your touch.
you grasp my shoulders then push down
as I let you take me under.

you were waiting for the bubbles to arise,
from my last breath
as waves pours over you
to take you under-shore
as I rise above.

coughing out water
as you reach out
for a hand
that was once reaching for you
that has left;

to never repeat
the accident
she has caused.

I hate you
and I hate how
I hurt everyone I love
and push everyone,
that doesn't know me
so they don't have to get hurt
as the others who were here before did
I don't mean to
I love you

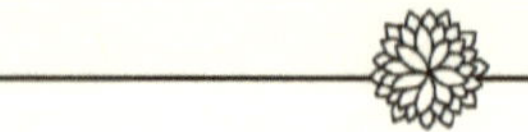

I screamed
I fought
I cried
to waste the time I had
on you
instead of the ones I loved
and cared for
that I called family.

I went for air,
as you pulled me under
into an abyss;
tone death-
with flutters of blinks.

You went for her
every time
when I tried to get you
and your attention,
it was her
it wasn't always her
you saw me for moments
but I guess you already had me
you had a pull
and you knew how to push

You took it from me
drained my lungs of air
made it so I was weak
pushed me over limits
so I would cry and cry
over and over again
you stole my voice
and captured it
and when you left
you kept it with you
hid it away
like you never hurt anyone
acted so innocent
when I confronted you.

To make your conscious be clean
and free of me
but my voice grew louder and louder
to where I can't be ignored!
my voice
went around and around
in your head
where your games couldn't be stopped
and you had to free me
from you.

You say you care
do you really?
you say you care even with clothes on
your goal is to get me without
I've tried to build something
to have it be broken down
to be grabbed
yet I still have it
to push you off is what I do
I can't let you in
to start sweet
was a lie.
you tried to take
anything you could get
your friends said I was "easy"
am I "easy" now?

It's the numb inside
that had torn you apart
that dug deeper than imagined.
pounding thoughts
that bring no emotion,

from evolving
from a sadness
that brought tears
and suffrage

to an abyss
that you hid in
with no escape

It hurt when you left
and I'm not sure if I should say thank you
because you saved me from myself
from falling in
and getting attached
I was venerable
but you were toxic
and when you left
it taught me that
in this world
there are more like you
and you were just one of them
that I fell in your trap

I'm lost without you
I don't know what to do

and I'm not so much as lonely
it's just a torn hole
that I have created myself
and I don't know where to find you

as maybe I am lost
or you have been found

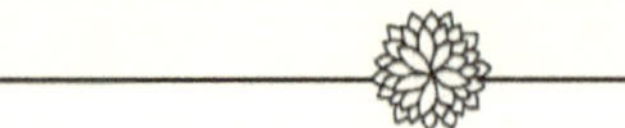

I was lost the day you left
the day my heart shattered
and the water was strained
 from my body.
when my legs trembled
and gravity had taken over.
where the swarm of thoughts
had overtaken my emotions.
that had drowned me
in toxic waters.
reaching above the waters
to seek a hand
that had led me to toxicity
in the pure beginning.
it was the moments I never had
when you weren't there

I am wasted—
a lost cause—
I fell under—
something untouchable hit me—

all you do is disfigure me
gash my heart out—
spill my organs
saw my bones.

you make me weak—
An Easy Target—

why do you haunt me?
as if I have ever done something to you.

as I lay there,
under the lifeless sky-
dark as midnight
as the snow lights up the ground-

Numbness, oversees my body (quiet)
as my mind detaches-
as if death stared me in the eyes.

warmth deceives with in me.

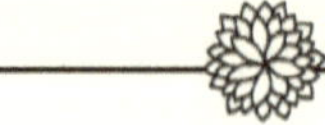

Growing Tree

You planted your seeds
as they grew into my veins,
as you watered me
and teased me with food
groomed me for a prize
as I let your seeds slip
and drift away.

You made me feel special
even though I was just a game

Even what we had
made me realize
we couldn't pop in and out
it was a while
but at a point
we stopped
and it hurt
when we were alone
and to come back
after years
wasn't fair
but we did
and things had changed
and there she was

You dragged me out
into an unknown world
made me feel loved
and wanted
then you throw me out
into unfamiliar streets
and left me to starve

It's fucked
when you deprived me
of happiness
of my choices
of my liberation

And I Laughed

Someone had told me you were nice
and I laughed.
I laughed because I didn't believe it
that you could genuinely care about someone
and I kept thinking
the thought was so unattainable
then you made me realize,
how I was treated meant nothing
and the thought that you could be nice
I didn't want to be thought
because you could never show me that
so I kept laughing
until it became so overwhelming
that I wanted you
but all along you could have been nice
but it was who I was that stopped it.

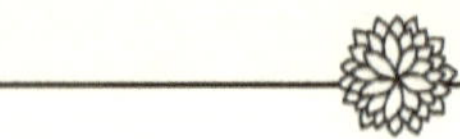

Your voice was never soothing to me
your hands were never able to stop me
you never had a hold on me
you did teach me very well
how to be sad
how to let go
and move on
and how to protect myself
when everyone else
had followed your lead

I'm not your baby.
I never was,
why you feel a need to call me that
and think that you get to see my body
because you want to?
I was never yours
and I never will be.
because who you have shown me
you're a heartless horny bastard.

And all I have ever wanted
was to cuddle up skin to skin,
falling asleep in your arms.

Craved

145

I craved the relationship
the photos,
the dates,
nights under the stars,
fighting over little things,
the attention,
the love
but never you.

I craved everything,
but never you.

I hid it away
what you did
had damaged me
and I left it
as if it never happened
it haunts me
I haven't forgotten
shoved it aside
till I felt better
and I can't move on

I couldn't love you
the chase was gone.
I told you before
the chase is the game.
and you're out.

It was all just teases
there was never a YOU
I just liked to believe there was
that everyone I had connected to
was a YOU
and they created this one YOU
but truth is I haven't found YOU yet
and I hope I never do

I wrote all the poems
thinking of you
when you didn't exist.

Epilogue

In the 8th grade I had wrote a spoken word poem to perform in class. After preforming this it made me realize that I love writing poetry. I actually wrote this about my sister as she was moving to college. I was also moving as my parents had split in 2010 and started living in separate housed in the year of 2013.

Summer of you

2014

When I was younger I waited for that car to roll up and you open the
door
I ran out calling your name as your arms open wide to hug me.

2 years later-
I stopped running-
I stopped calling your name-
I went to the car and saw our mom

"Are you packed?" she always asked.
"Yeah"

Driving down the open highway,
windows down and our song playing.
I would sing my heart out-
over- and over- and over again.

I got out and heard my name just like I used to do.
the open pool, we swam all day
it was time to go.

I got home and you were waiting,
We grabbed the volleyball and went to the park
Me falling like a bird trying to fly for the first time.
You ran to get the ball.

Another year past
I went out to get that old beat up volleyball
Failing to hit-
You didn't come-
You weren't there-

The laughing stopped.
Silence-
That's all I heard
Silence-
Silence, silence, silence
That can't be all,
You can't leave me like this.
No not again.

Day by day
Week by week
Month by month
No car door-
No more running up
No more calling your name
No arms to run into
No you-

That's when summer ended
"Goodbye"

About the Author

Alexis Nicole has a bachelor of Arts in Anthropology. Has been writing poems since she was 10 years old starting out with a poem, "Bench" for an elementary assignment, and continued using poetry as a coping mechanism battling anxiety and depression throughout high school and college. Now trying to navigate life and her career.

Instagram:
Business: @H.AlexisNicole
Personal: @Mightylex

www.ingramcontent.com/pod-product-compliance
Lightning Source LLC
Chambersburg PA
CBHW021211160726
47994CB00001B/434